This book is dedicated to the little person in each of us.
May all our journeys be supported so that we can create
vibrant inner worlds that liberate our outer world.
—CMC

To the young hearts who seek the magic
beyond what is material and understand that
life is more than meets the eye.
—SZ

CRYSTAL
McCREARY

Illustrations by
SONALI ZOHRA

YOU ARE A RAINBOW
OF ENERGY

A Kid's Guide to the Chakras

Gibbs Smith

Did you know that you are a rainbow?
Yes, you are!

You may have pink skin or brown, black hair or even blue, but know that you make up every color and hue of the rainbow. How lucky that you have this book with ancient wisdom from the yoga tradition (a very old practice from India and Africa used for living our best lives). It will help you see the *true* you.

For starters, you are a human being. This means you are made of the obvious stuff like skin, bones, a little muscle, a little fat, and vital organs like a beating heart and lungs that breathe. Yet deep beneath all these fleshy body parts, you are also **ENERGY**.

That is what this book is all about: the seven energy centers in your body that affect how you feel, think, and act. The ancient yogis (people who practice yoga) called these energy centers **CHAKRAS**. Each chakra has a color and a location in your body. Together, they make a glorious rainbow bridge. Our prana, or life force, travels along this bridge. Feelings, sensations, thoughts, experiences, memories, and actions come from the chakra energy centers, too. This book will help you keep your rainbow bridge in tip-top shape so your amazing life force can travel through your body without any traffic jams.

The coolest thing about learning about your chakras is that when you do, you will see much more than your body, skin, and hair. You will see and feel the rainbow of colors inside yourself and in everyone around you!

A NOTE FOR YOUNG READERS: When you first begin learning about the chakras, you will need the help of someone older to learn all the new words. Read this book together, then you both can explore the activities

1
ROOT
CHAKRA
Safety

2
SACRAL
CHAKRA
Creativity

3
SOLAR PLEXUS
CHAKRA
Confidence

4
HEART
CHAKRA
Love

5
THROAT
CHAKRA
Expression

6
THIRD EYE
CHAKRA
Intuition

7
CROWN
CHAKRA
Connection

and practices. You can do the practices in any order you like. On some days, you might prefer to have a quiet practice with just poses and softly spoken affirmations. On others, you might want to be loud and do only the Make Some Noise practices. Sometimes you might want to do everything at once. Be sure to ask for help with the practices when you need it. Once you are familiar with the poses and the words, you may choose to practice on your own in a quiet place at home.

Just like a rainbow, our adventure starts with the first chakra and the color red, located at the very base of the spine—the bones along the center of your back that help you stretch, shrink, twist, bend, arch, and round your back. Then we travel up the spine to the colors orange, yellow, green, blue, indigo, and finally violet. Can you see the rainbow bridge yet? If not, you will soon.

Let's begin!

1st Chakra

*Green light, yellow light, red light...
stop: let's begin here with the glowing
red light at the base of your spine.*

NAME
Root Chakra

LOCATION
Root (base of the spine)

SANSKRIT NAME
Muladhara ("moolah-thAA-ruh")

COLOR
Red

ELEMENT
Earth

Everybody feels worried or scared sometimes. When fear takes over, sometimes the mind races with thoughts! These thoughts can get in the way and make it hard to think clearly or concentrate, but it's important to remember that you have tools.

The earth and your body are always there and can help! Take a deep breath and press your feet down into the earth, the floor, or whatever surface they are touching. You are here, fully alive, standing strong, with the ground supporting you.

Squatting Frog Pose

Sink low toward the grounding earth; breathe deep and feel heat in your seat as you squat like a frog!

1 Take your shoes off. Step your feet wide apart. Press your feet into the floor.

2 Sink your hips down between your heels. Bring your fists or palms together in front of your heart. Press your elbows against your inner knees. Take two or three full breaths.

3 Take your Frog Pose for a few hops until you feel settled, then try again. Notice the feeling of being close to the ground. Do you feel heavy or light? Active or relaxed? Notice the sensations of heat building in your body and say where they are.

Let's Make Some Noise!
The sound for the Root Chakra is LAM.
Stretch each sound of the word as
you say, **"LLLAAAMMM!"**

Say It Loud, and Say It Proud

My body is strong, and so am I. I love my body, and I listen
to its wisdom. I am alive and have a right to be here.

2nd Chakra

As you rock and roll, feel the warm orange glow flow up your spine from your pelvic bowl!

NAME
Sacral Chakra

LOCATION
Sacrum (bone at the back of the pelvis)

SANSKRIT NAME
Svadhisthana ("svAA-thiSH-TAA-nuh")

COLOR
Orange

ELEMENT
Water

Sometimes big emotions can feel overwhelming, like we are little boats in a giant storm! Imagine yourself as a boat with an anchor. The anchor that can help keep you steady is your body and your breath. Drop your anchor: feel the parts of you that touch the ground and take a deep breath. Breathe and feel the ground for a few moments to connect to the steadiness inside you.

Now picture the back, the sides, and the front of your pelvis. It is shaped just like a bowl. Place your hands around the sides of your hips and feel the bowl. Take a few breaths and imagine a warm orange light filling that bowl.

Seated Cat-Cow Pose

Rock and roll your back like a cat; let the waves of your spine soothe the swirling, twirling feelings that need attention and care.

1 Sit in a comfortable position.

2 Inhale, lift your head, and arch your back. Exhale, scoop your tail under, tuck your chin, and round your back like a cat.

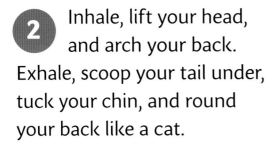

3 Move with a smooth rhythm, as if a gentle river flows up and down with your spine. Keep breathing and let your spine ride the gentle waves of your breath.

Let's Make Some Noise!
The sound for the Sacral Chakra is VAM.
Stretch each sound of the word as you say, "VVVAAAMMM!"

Say It Loud, and Say It Proud
My emotions are real and valid. I deserve to feel good!
I care for myself and say, "No, I don't like that," or
"Please stop," or "I need more space," when others
do things that make me uncomfortable.

3rd Chakra

*Heat up your center and feel strong
and powerful from the inside out!*

NAME

Solar Plexus Chakra

LOCATION

Navel (belly button)

SANSKRIT NAME

Manipura ("money-poo-ruh")

COLOR

Yellow

ELEMENT

Fire

Do you know how powerful you are? You can do ANYTHING your heart desires! Just focus your attention, take one step at a time, and don't give up. YOU are the boss of you.

Boat Pose

*Doing hard things and challenging yourself
builds strength and confidence and helps you grow!*

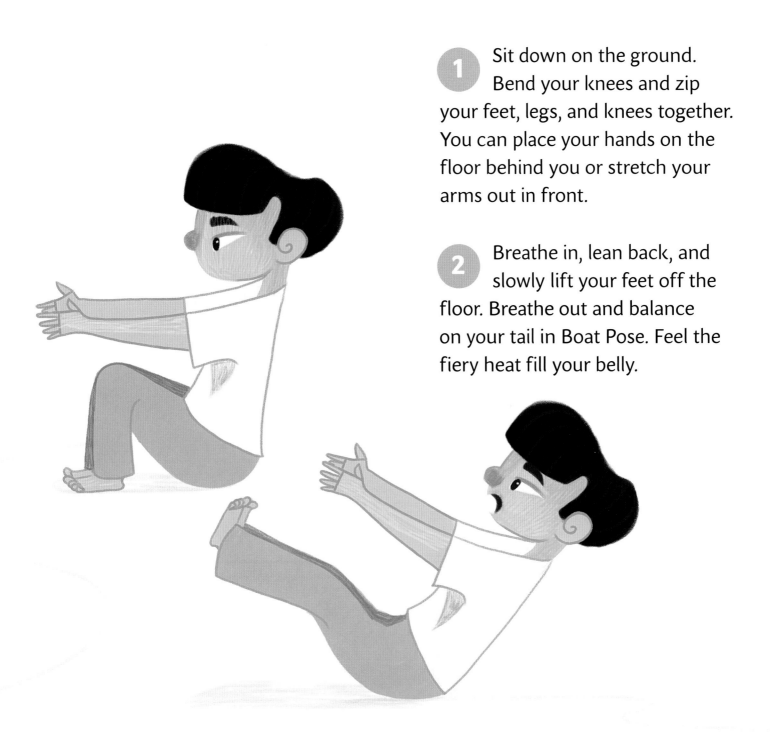

1 Sit down on the ground. Bend your knees and zip your feet, legs, and knees together. You can place your hands on the floor behind you or stretch your arms out in front.

2 Breathe in, lean back, and slowly lift your feet off the floor. Breathe out and balance on your tail in Boat Pose. Feel the fiery heat fill your belly.

Let's Make Some Noise!
The sound for the Naval Chakra is RAM.
Turn your vocal power on and say,
"RRRAAAMMM!"

Say It Loud, and Say It Proud
I am powerful! I can do
anything I set my mind to!

4th Chakra

*Let your green light shine
from your heart!*

NAME

Heart Chakra

LOCATION

Heart (center of chest)

SANSKRIT NAME

Anahata ("un-AA-huh-Thuh")

COLOR

Green

ELEMENT

Air

There is a part of you that always knows just what to do—in an argument, a fight, when you know you are wrong, or when you know you are right. Take a deep breath and let yourself walk in the other person's shoes. Feel what they feel. Then listen to your heart. It will guide you to the caring thing to do!

Cobra Pose

Open your chest wide; feel and connect to others
in a big-hearted and caring way.

1 Lie down on your belly. Place your hands alongside your lower ribs. Press your hands, feet, and hips into the ground.

2 Breathe in and gently lift your head, neck, and chest.

3 Breathe out and lower everything back down. Do this a few times, lifting your Cobra head and heart as you inhale. Exhale as you lower your Cobra.

Let's Make Some Noise!
The sound for the Heart Chakra is YAM.
Say it loud and proud: **"YYYAAAMMM!"**

Say It Loud, and Say It Proud
I am lovable. I am loving to myself and others.
When in doubt, I listen to and trust my heart.

5th Chakra

Let your words be bathed in cool, clear, blue light!

NAME

Throat Chakra

LOCATION

Throat (front of neck)

SANSKRIT NAME

Vishuddha ("vish-shoo-thee")

COLOR

Bright Blue

ELEMENT

Sound (music)

When you feel shy, it takes time to feel safe enough to share your thoughts. Sometimes, thoughts that are clear in your mind can come out jumbled and confused! Clear your Throat Chakra to speak clearly and truthfully.

Lion's Breath Pose

*Speak it, growl it, roar it, or shout it;
just be sure your voice shares
what's true for you!*

1. Sit on your heels or in another comfortable position.

2. Open your mouth wide and stick out your tongue.

3. Breathe in and then roar like an angry lion in the jungle with the biggest "AHHH" sound you can make! Do that three times and see how it feels to let your voice be heard.

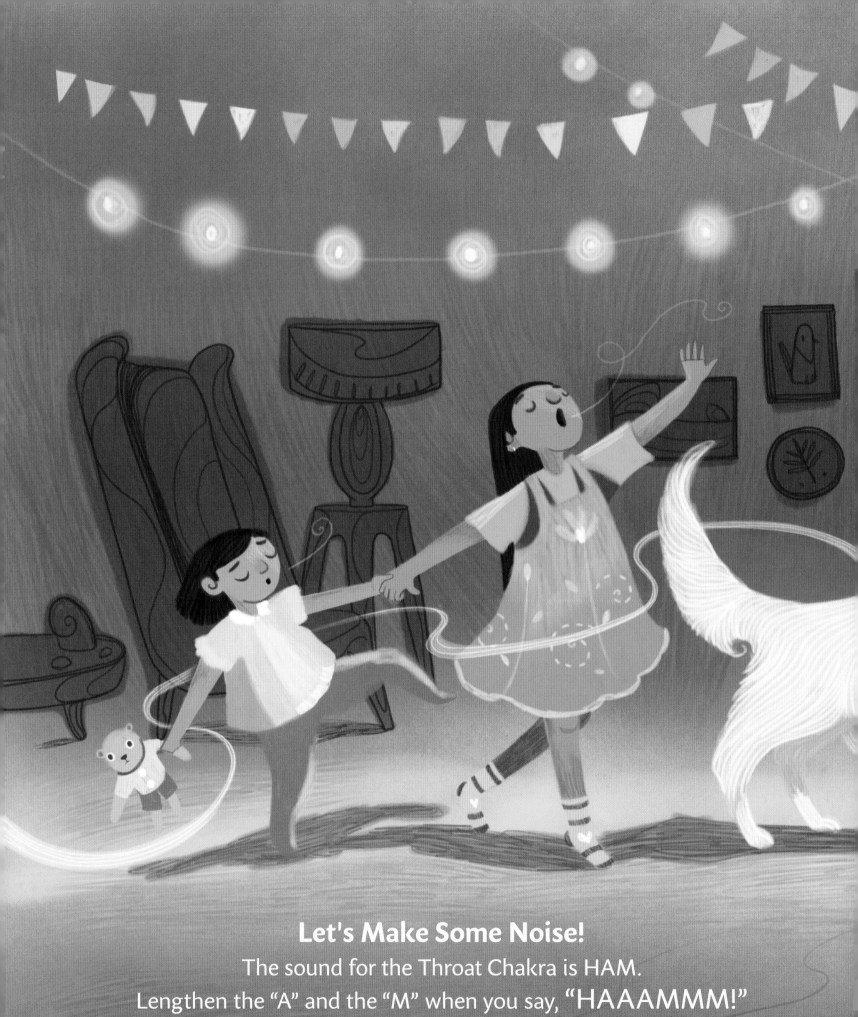

Let's Make Some Noise!
The sound for the Throat Chakra is HAM.
Lengthen the "A" and the "M" when you say, "HAAAMMM!"

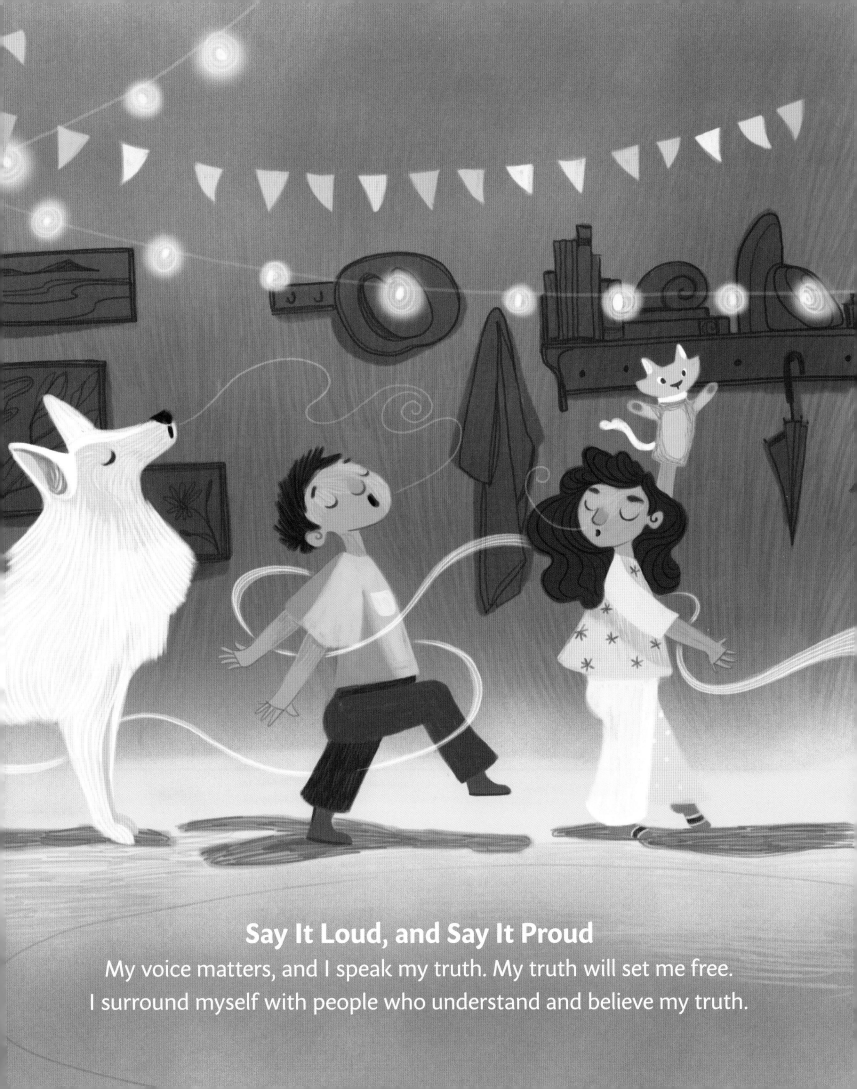

Say It Loud, and Say It Proud

My voice matters, and I speak my truth. My truth will set me free.
I surround myself with people who understand and believe my truth.

6th Chakra

Deep, dark indigo helps the imagination flow!

NAME
Third Eye Chakra

LOCATION
Third Eye (center of forehead)

SANSKRIT NAME
Ajna ("AAg-nyuh")

COLOR
Indigo

ELEMENT
Light

Being forgetful or having trouble picturing ideas can be frustrating. This part of the rainbow helps with memory and imagination.

Take a deep breath and watch the cool blue light of the Throat Chakra turn to a dark blue (called indigo) as you move up to the "third eye" in your forehead. This dark blue chakra is truly a place of clarity and insight.

Child's Pose

Curl up inside your personal cocoon and rest;
then emerge full of bright, beautiful, and creative ideas!

1 Sit on your heels.

2 Open your knees wide and walk your hands forward.

3 Place your forehead on the floor and rest. Take a few breaths. Gently roll your head from side to side. Give your forehead a gentle massage.

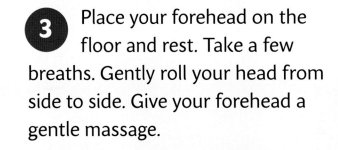

Let's Make Some Noise!
The sound for the Brow Chakra is AUM.
Raise your voice again and stretch the "A," "U,"
and "M" when you say, "AAAUUUMMM!"

Say It Loud, and Say It Proud
I observe and see things in my life clearly.
In tough times, I know things will get better.
I sit and I wait until I know what to do.

7th Chakra

*Royal violet light
is your birthright!*

NAME
Crown Chakra

LOCATION
Crown (top of your head)

SANSKRIT NAME
Sahasrara ("suh-huss-rAA-ruh")

COLOR
Violet

ELEMENT
Thought

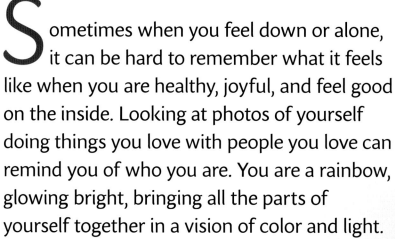

Sometimes when you feel down or alone, it can be hard to remember what it feels like when you are healthy, joyful, and feel good on the inside. Looking at photos of yourself doing things you love with people you love can remind you of who you are. You are a rainbow, glowing bright, bringing all the parts of yourself together in a vision of color and light.

Take a full breath as you imagine the dark indigo light from your Third Eye Chakra turning to violet, a vibrant purple hue, as you move up to your Crown Chakra. This color expands beyond your head as if you are wearing a large, regal crown.

Take three to five breaths. As you sit, imagine zooming out as you look at yourself through a camera lens. Take in the full view.

You are a rainbow.

Wide-Legged Standing Pose

Let your strength, power, and truth fill the room with all the colors and beauty of the brightest rainbow bridge!

1 Stand with your feet wide apart.

2 Fold forward and place your hands on the floor shoulder-width apart.

3 Release the top of your head to the ground. If it doesn't touch the ground, place a block (or a book or two) in front of you to bring the ground up to your head. Take five deep breaths, feeling your head connect to the surface it touches.

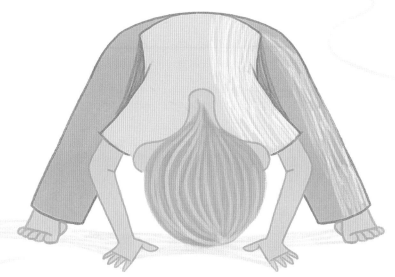

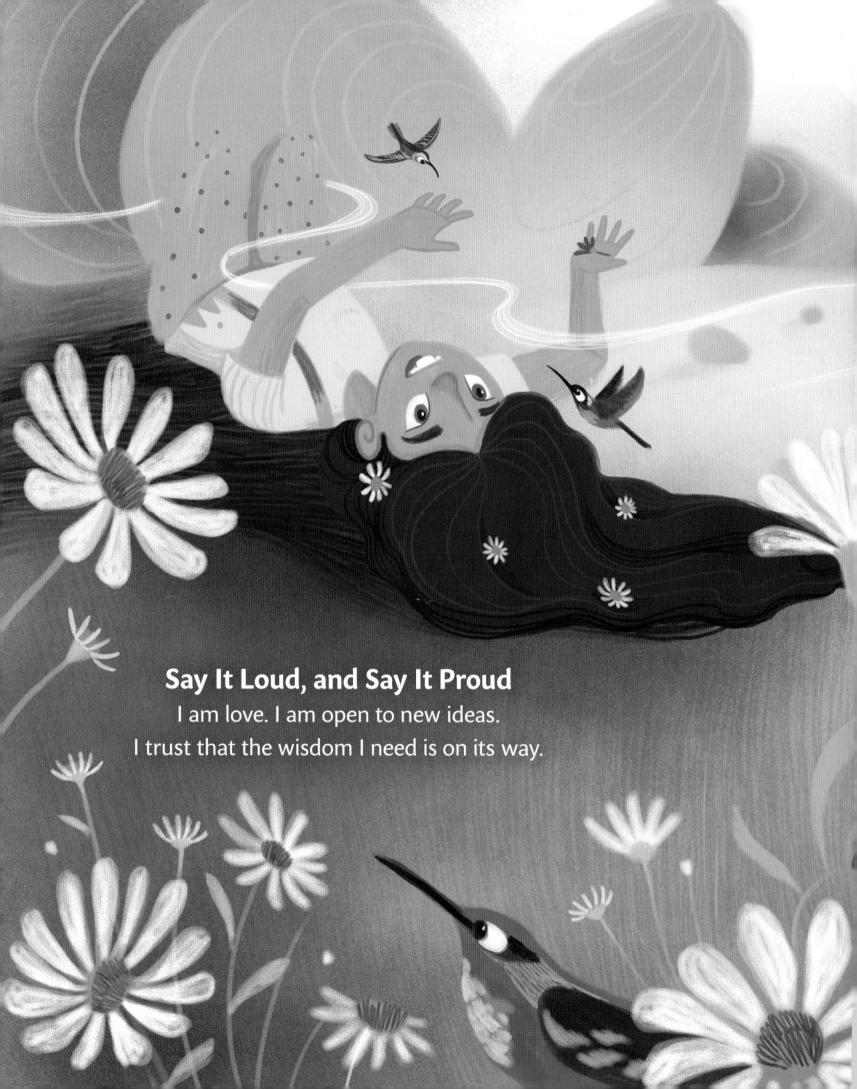

Say It Loud, and Say It Proud
I am love. I am open to new ideas.
I trust that the wisdom I need is on its way.

Now It's Time to Get Quiet

Close your eyes and visualize the beautiful rainbow in you. Can you see, feel, hear, touch, and taste all the colors of the rainbow that make you *you*?

A Little Chakra History and Science

The word **CHAKRA** means *wheel* in the ancient language called Sanskrit. The ancient yogis who spoke Sanskrit and lived in India more than 3,000 years ago believed that balancing these constantly spinning wheels of energy was an important part of healthy living. They taught that taking care of your chakra energy helps you stay healthy, smart, and strong, just like getting a good night's sleep and eating nutritious foods do. The energy from your chakras has a big effect on your emotions, your thoughts, your actions, and all your experiences with others. So understanding the chakras can help you feel better about yourself and the world around you.

Some scientists agree with the wisdom passed down by the ancient yogis. These scientists noticed that the bundles of nerves found along the spine were located in similar places to the main chakra centers. Nerves contain tiny bits of information that our five senses gather from the world around us. This information travels through the nervous system along the spine to the brain. Here, it is translated into a to-do list for the body, like "Hand, move away from the hot stove *now*!"

How to Balance Your Chakra Energy at Home

In the beginning, you will have to pay very close attention to the feelings in your body (sensations) and your mind (emotions). Being curious and paying close attention to feelings will help you notice when your chakra energy is moving slowly—like rush-hour traffic—and when you may need to boost your energy in one chakra area or another. For example, regular stomachaches might be your Navel Chakra telling you that your belly needs better

food or care. Constant headaches are often the body's way of telling you that you need to pay some attention to stress (feeling overwhelmed) or nutrition (healthy foods). Here are some tips for giving your chakras a regular tune-up so that these spinning wheels can turn easily and pass energy along through your body:

+ Daily yoga practice
+ Slow, deep breathing in and out of your nose
+ Eating "the rainbow," or lots of different colored foods at every meal
+ Drinking lots of water (instead of sugary drinks)
+ Daily exercise like walking, running, jumping rope, dancing to your favorite songs, or playing a sport

Crystal McCreary is a coach, health educator, and yoga and mindfulness educator and teacher trainer.

Crystal is the author of the *Little Yogi Deck: Simple Practices to Help Kids Move through Big Emotions* (Bala Kids 2021). She is also on the faculty at the Kripalu Center for Yoga and Health. Crystal currently works as a health and wellness educator at a K-12 independent school in New York City while studying to become a psychotherapist in the Mental Health Counseling program at City University of New York–Hunter.

She loves working with people to help them uncover their gifts, lead with creativity and love, and source vitality and play while navigating demanding lives. Learn more about Crystal at crystalmccreary.com.

Sonali Zohra is an illustrator/author based in British Columbia, Canada. Her work is inspired by her love of nature, philosophy, myth, and spirituality. She has illustrated several books over the years and is the author of *I Dream of Ganesha* (Bala Kids, 2024). To see more of her work visit sonalizohra.com.

First Edition

29 28 27 26 25   5 4 3 2 1

Text © 2025 Crystal McCreary
Illustrations © 2025 Sonali Zohra

Published by

Gibbs Smith

570 N. Sportsplex Dr.

Kaysville, Utah 84037

1.800.835.4993 orders

www.gibbs-smith.com

Designed by Ryan Thomann
Manufactured in Guangdong, China, in November 2024 by RRD Asia Printing Solutions.

This product is made of FSC®-certified and other controlled material.

Library of Congress Cataloging-in-Publication Data: 2024940275
ISBN: 978-1-4236-6565-6